T0131662

FEMINIST REFLECTIONS ON MISSION AND LEADERSHIP

A Uniting Church Minister's perspective

JAN REEVE

WESTBOW
PRESS®
A DIVISION OF THOMAS NELSON
& ZONDERVAN

WestBow Press books may be ordered through booksellers or by contacting:

WestBow Press
A Division of Thomas Nelson & Zondervan
1663 Liberty Drive
Bloomington, IN 47403
www.westbowpress.com
844-714-3454

Scripture quotations marked NRSV are from the New Revised Standard Version Bible, copyright © 1989 the Division of Christian Education of the National Council of the Churches of Christ in the United States of America. Used by permission. All rights reserved.

ISBN: 978-1-6642-5599-9 (sc)
ISBN: 978-1-6642-5600-2 (hc)
ISBN: 978-1-6642-5598-2 (e)

Library of Congress Control Number: 2022901522

Print information available on the last page.

WestBow Press rev. date: 02/16/2022

DEDICATION

For my mum Gwen who encouraged me to go forward
into wherever God was leading me, thank
you for your faithful life.

This book is dedicated to all the women who have
humbly served Jesus Christ in their lives
especially those who trailblazed leadership
within the Christian Church.

For those who continue to live out their
calling with the joy and privilege
this is, regardless of their reception—keep on the journey!!

CONTENTS

INTRODUCTION

Feminist reflections on mission and leadership: Where have we been and how are we travelling?

The development of this book has been in my mind and heart for many years. As a woman Minister of the Word of the Uniting Church in Australia New South Wales/Australian Capital Territory (NSW/ACT) Synod, I have been looking back on twenty-five years of ministry formation and ministry experience within the Uniting Church. During the time of my studies for my Master of Ministry degree back in 2008, there was a growing desire in me to continue to grow and be equipped for my ongoing ministry, which began back in 1994 as a candidate. The rapid rate of social change and the continuing relocation of the church from the centre of society in the Christendom model of church to the margins of society, have continued throughout Australia since the 1990s, but even more so in the 2000s and beyond

I am amazed that in the current social and political context in Australia, I am finalising this book against a huge backdrop of outrage by women about ill treatment and violence against women across society. This has exploded and needs addressing by all governments and organisations, and requires deep reflection on basic respect for gender equality and people's value as equals.

Many people have come and gone in ministry, even within the time of my service. It is interesting to look back and observe with hindsight the ways in which we, as part of the church institution, have been slow to accept and respond to the impact of social change and shifting values.

One of the strengths that has been evident in this time of rapid social change is the way in which women have found their rightful place in ministry leadership in a variety of church settings. Women have their unique gifting and calling, which is equally as valid and valuable as it is for men whom God has called. Having grown up in the 1960s and 1970s in Australia as a child of the women's liberation era, it is not surprising that my pathway into adulthood and ministry has been about permission-giving for women. This period also saw lobbying for significant changes in church practices due to the re-discovery of Jesus's ministry with women and the rise of the feminist theological movement in the 1980s and 1990s.

For those who are in the first half of life today, this may seem irrelevant or unnecessary to recall. Much of that change has been embraced and forms the foundation and practices of our world and church today. Indeed, other organisations within society, including political organisations and business and community services organisations (or parts of them) continue to support women in leadership on many levels, although the glass ceiling still seems hard to break in many places. That is not to say that all is well, or there isn't room for improvement or renewal, but women in many spheres are much better off in terms of access and equity than they were forty years ago.

For those in the second half of life, there is much to be remembered and shared about the journey that has taken place, and the wisdom and lessons that have been learnt, in order to create a future that is life-giving and Christ-centred. For those who have the privilege of leadership in the mission of God to lead the church into the future, I hope that these reflections will encourage you to understand the past and how we've come to the present time. I also hope that it will enable you who are younger to persevere as you have the challenge of creating the future church.

So, drawing on some of my earlier thinking in this field, which I am passionate about, I offer these reflections on the mission of God and the leadership of the church through my feminist lens. I hope this will encourage, mobilise, and affirm all of those who believe in the wholeness that comes from being united with Jesus Christ in his life, death, and resurrection and lead to the transformation of the world person by person and community by community.

All biblical quotations in this book come from the New Revised Standard Version of the Bible (NRSV).

Women are equally created by God, redeemed by Christ...equally called to mission in this world...
Elizabeth Johnson

CHAPTER 1

Feminist perspectives on God and the mission of Jesus

As I begin to discuss the relationships between feminist perspectives and God's mission, it is essential to define these areas in order to highlight some key links between them, and how they have enabled the Christian Church to fulfil its call to extend the reign of God into the world God loves. Feminist insights encompass a large body of theological literature, which has been produced especially over the past forty years. This literature critiques traditional understandings of God, church, and mission from a feminist perspective. There are a wide variety of feminist theologies that have developed, not just one exact view. It will be some of these theologies and the history of Christian mission from New Testament times that I will explore.

Elizabeth Johnson, in her thorough exploration of God from a feminist perspective, defines feminist theology broadly as,

a reflection on God and all things in the light of God that stands consciously in the company of all the world's women, explicitly prizing their genuine humanity while uncovering and criticizing its persistent violation in sexism, itself an omnipresent paradigm of unjust relationships. In terms of Christian doctrine, this perspective claims the fullness of the religious heritage for women precisely as human, in their own right and independent from personal identification with men. Women are equally created in the image of God, equally redeemed by Christ, equally sanctified by the Holy Spirit; women are equally involved in the ongoing tragedy of sin and the mystery of grace, equally called to mission in this world, equally destined for life with God in glory. [1]

The mission of God is a general term which relates to the way in which God has been revealed to humanity in history in the person of Jesus of Nazareth. In his life and ministry, people were led into the fullness of life with God, in relationship with God, by faith. As David Bosch puts it,

> missio Dei, (God's mission) is God's self-revelation as the One who loves the world, God's involvement in and with the world, the nature and activity of God, which embraces both the church and the world, and in which the church is privileged to participate. Missio Dei enunciates the good news that God is a God -for -people. [2]

I offer my own definition of mission, which has been strongly influenced by feminist insights over a number of years. Mission is an activity in which God and humankind work together to improve life and help others discover God's mercy and grace, leading to personal and social transformation. Sharing the good news of God's love in word and action through Jesus the Christ enables God's justice, healing, purpose for life, and all creation to become possible.

The first feminist insight is in our understanding of God and

---

[1] Johnson, E, *She Who Is*, 8.
[2] Bosch, D. J., *Transforming Mission*. (New York, 1993). 10

God's identity as a God of mission. God's identity and our Christian understanding of God as a trinity is a key to discovering God's very nature as relational, a trinity of Father, Son, and Spirit, bound together in love and purpose. This varies greatly from the more hierarchical understandings that we have from traditional theology. Judi Long puts it this way:

> the Father, Son, and Spirit are distinct, are 3 persons and yet one God, Son and Spirit proceeding from the Father and each with particular work to do. They are seen as male, authoritarian, rational, transcendent, changeless, as opposed to a feminist view of relational, loving, dynamic and immanent. [3]

A feminist understanding of the Trinity is based on a mutual equality within God, meaning that God is a community of equals. It points to patterns of differentiation that are non-hierarchical, and to forms of relating that do not involve dominance. [4] This highlights the God who is searching, is seeking to be in a relationship with humanity, and is motivated by love. This enables us to discern that Christian mission is based on seeking and developing positive relationships, is at the core of God's purpose, and reflects the God who calls us into the world. We are called to be in relationship with God, with others, and with the creation for which we are carers and custodians. [5]

Feminist insights have enabled other language about God involving feminine imagery to be developed. Metaphors like mother and sister, as well as explorations of scripture that have reclaimed the feminine images of God as Spirit from Proverbs Chapter 1,

---

[3] Long J "Miss-iology meets Ms-Theology: Missiology and Feminist theology in creative interaction." *Mission Studies,* (2002) *Vol XIX, No 1-37,* 167

[4] Johnson, E, *She Who Is,* 219.

[5] Long J, Miss-iology meets Ms-Theology 166

are revealing. The Spirit *Ruach and Shekinah* (Exodus 25:8) are reclaimed as female images for the work of God in the world and the presence of God with the people. [6] Non-gender specific language has also been developed to help expand our images of God beyond gender, such as creator, redeemer and sanctifier; lover, loved, and love. Co-shared imagery is also used, as in messenger, pilgrim, and healer, or with interpersonal images such as marriage and dance, within the relationship of the godhead.

Explorations of the divine Son, the *logos*, the word of God, have been expanded as the Christ has been identified as the wisdom of God, a feminine image for Jesus. His ministry and mission is full of barrier-crossing for women. Jesus's ministry challenged the patriarchal bias of his culture and has been overwhelming in elevating the status and value of women in the first century and to this time. Gloria Dharmaraj comments on the significance of the incarnation:

> The family story of God sending Jesus as a missionary to the world, namely, the story of Incarnation is a border crossing event. The word became flesh and lived among us, and we have seen his glory (John 1:14). [7]

The second area in which feminist insights and mission are connected is in the ministry and mission of Jesus of Nazareth. Jesus's ministry is summed up in Luke's vision: to bring sight to the blind, to bring good news to the poor, to set free those who are captive, to comfort the broken-hearted, and to proclaim the time of God's favour. "Luke 4 (NRSV)." These were all clearly embodied in Jesus's ministry to women. This began with Mary, his mother, who acted

---

[6] Johnson, E, 85

[7] Dharmaraj, G. E., "Women as border crossing agents: transforming the center from the margins." 1998 *Missiology 26:1*, 56

on the promises of God, who shared her joy and the message of liberation of the poor with Elizabeth, her cousin celebrating the joy of being raised up for a special purpose. Luke 1 (NRSV)

Jesus's ministry involved a number of women who supported him and his co-workers in various ways. Some of these, including Mary Magdalene, Joanna (the wife of Chuza), Susanna, and Salome (Zebedee's wife and mother of James and John), are mentioned in Luke 8. Jesus included many women as followers, even though they are not named as part of the group of twelve. Mary and Martha of Bethany, sisters of Lazarus, are unique in that they show Jesus crossing cultural and religious boundaries as a rabbi and teaching women privately. He also taught many who were amongst the crowds that often gathered to hear him proclaim God's message. We hear of these sisters several times and are aware of their profound faith in Jesus through the experience of the death of their brother Lazarus and his later resurrection.

The confessions of Martha and Mary of Bethany reveal strong faith in Jesus as the Christ. They are both profound theological statements, unlike most others of the official male disciples at the time. According to Sook Ja Chung, "there was no doubt about the missionary roles played by Mary and Martha, especially in the case of Martha whom John agreed to introduce as an important faith confessing woman (John 11:27)." [8]

The mission of Jesus also involved crossing social boundaries with women and children who were ill or who, through healing sick, frail, and dying people, became ritually unclean. Men of that time would never do this work. They left many things like caring for the sick, the frail, and the dead to women. Women would fulfill those rites, but then be unable to participate in the community until they were purified under the requirements of the law. Some examples include the bleeding woman who touched Jesus's cloak (Matthew

---

[8] Chung, Sook Ja, "Bible Study: Women's ways of doing mission in the story of Mary and Martha" *International Review of Mission. 2004,* Vol 93 Iss 368, p12

9), the girl who died and was brought back to life (Matthew 9), the foreign woman who asked for bread for her children (Mark 7), and the woman of Samaria at the well (John 4). These show Jesus crossing cultural and religious barriers to accept women, and value and care for them in a way that was radical in patriarchal Judaism. Some feminist theologians are troubled by Jesus as a male Saviour for women, but when we consider "the way in which he redefined the status of women, and embraced a vision of a renewed order of equality, no woman of the time could have achieved that other than by the plan and purpose of God." [9]

When Jesus approached the city of David prior to his arrest, he mourned the loss of those who would not accept him as God's Messiah. In Luke's gospel it is recorded that Jesus said, "O Jerusalem, Jerusalem, you slay the prophets and stone those who are sent to you. How often have I wanted to gather your children as a mother hen gathers her chicks under her wings but you refused me." "Luke 13:34 (NRSV)" The feminine image of Jesus-Sophia, the wisdom of God, and the mother hen are very powerful. Elizabeth Schussler Fiorenza notes that "these were signs of the new order, the reign of God, recorded within the gospels that Jesus brought about and carried a new depth of meaning revealing a feminist perspective." [10]

Feminist insights can play a large part in expanding our understanding of mission, both in its origins and in its ongoing practice in the history of the Christian Church. The mission of God is a profoundly human and humanizing commitment and activity. Therefore, its scope, properly understood, will critique, redress, and transform that which is not life-giving, including sexism. How did this continue to unfold in the history of the early church? The next chapter will explore his and the continued participation of women in the early church.

---

[9] Long, J, (2002) *Miss-iology...*, p160

[10] 12 Schussler Fiorenza, E, *In Memory of Her* (London, 1983) 134

"The cosmic vision of feminism is not an illusory dream ...it is the vision of the gospel"
Patricia Wilson-Kastner

CHAPTER 2

Reflections on the participation of women leaders in Church history.

T he most significant event in the mission of Jesus of Nazareth was his death and resurrection. We see in these events the power of sacrificial love and the triumph over the forces of alienation for all humanity. Patricia Wilson Kastner comments on the significance of Jesus's life when she says,

> God has assured us that such healing has entered the world through the Spirit and is at work among us and that this is the promise that God is fulfilling among us. The cosmic vision of feminism is not an illusory dream of naïve individuals, but in its most thoroughgoing and radical form is the vision of the gospel, the promise made by God to the world through Jesus Christ. [11]

Among the many women who followed Jesus, Mary Magdalene was their leader, privileged with others to be the first witness to

---

[11] Wilson Kastner, P, *Faith, Feminism and the Christ.* (Philadelphia, 1983) 114

Jesus's resurrection. It is the privilege of being the apostle to the apostles, as Augustine so rightly named her, which began the ongoing missionary endeavour of those who followed Jesus and who, later in houses and synagogues, worshipped him as Messiah. Jesus's post-resurrection statement to Mary Magdalene proclaimed a new relationship between those who are believers, based on their inclusion by God. They were to relate to one another as brothers and sisters in a family. He said "go to my brothers and say to them, I am ascending to my Father and your Father, to my God and your God." "John 20:17 (NRSV)." Those who were previously masters and slaves became sisters and brothers in Christ, just as they became daughters and sons of God. [12] This was a particular challenge for the early Christians, who began to live in a new way in their communities that would challenge the surrounding Jewish culture.

Other areas of exploration of feminist perspectives in the early church were the role of the Holy Spirit in mission and the later history of Christian mission. The beginning of the mission of the church was Jesus's instruction to go into all the world and be witnesses for Christ in the known and unknown territories. Waiting for the baptism of the Holy Spirit, which would give the disciples great power, was a time of transition and community-building among them. In the Pentecost event, we saw how the Spirit *Ruach* (Hebrew feminine) was poured out with fire, wind, languages and wonder, to be the advocate and counsellor that would work with them in mission. *Ruach-Spirit Sophia* has come to renew all of creation, beginning with humankind.

The role and importance of the Holy Spirit has been reclaimed in more recent years in western theology as the third and often unspoken person of the Trinity. Considering the importance of Christ's call for the disciples to wait for the Spirit to be outpoured

---

[12] Lienemann-Perrin, C, "The Biblical Foundation ... *International Review of Mission,* (2004) Vol 93, Iss 368, 27

and to fulfil the prophecy of Joel, the feminine roots of the Spirit may be part of the reason why the Spirit had not been given equal standing or signified importance in the Trinity, instead relegated to being referred to as *it*. In the Hebrew understanding of *Shekinah*, there is an identification of the Spirit as feminine, as *she*. In early Christianity, the Spirit was symbolised as the hovering mother bird, the Spirit connected with bringing new life into being. The figure of the dove in Christian art was linked to the Greek view of the dove as a symbol of the goddess of love, Aphrodite. The Spirit was understood as the symbol of divine female power. [13] The idea of the Holy Spirit evolved into the Mother church and later to Mary, the mother of Jesus the Christ and Mary the mother of God, *theotokos* in Catholic theology. [14]

The role of women in the mission of the apostolic church was varied, but women played an active role in both the private and public spheres of the new Christian communities that arose. Worship in Jerusalem centred on the Temple and the understanding of the Pentecost event enabled people to accept that men and women, old and young, were all filled with God's Spirit and that women could play their part in worship. "As the public gathering of the ecclesia of believers in Christ took place in homes and saw itself as a family-style community, its organization was well-suited to giving women the chance to actively participate."[15]

Once the church mission to the gentiles began with Paul and his journeys, many women were named and acknowledged as leaders of the church in their towns. These women included Phoebe, Lydia, Prisca, Mary, Tryphaena, Tryphosa, Persis, and Junia. It seems that the work in a non-Jewish setting enabled the role of women in the

---

[13] Johnson, E, *She Who Is* (New York,1992). 84

[14] Johnson, 86

[15] Lienemann-Perrin, C, 18-19

church's mission to expand, in a way that was limited amongst Jewish Christian communities.

> The decision of the church at Antioch, moved by the Spirit, to redefine theologically the traditional categories of male and female opened the door to equal rights for women in leading worship, in the life of house communities and also in spreading the faith beyond the city itself, as travelling missionaries, although to a limited extent. [16]

By the end of the second century, women's freedom to engage publicly in mission had been squashed. According to Lienemann-Perrin,

> What was especially fateful for women's mission was that their share in responsibility for public proclamation, the teaching of the church, baptism and the eucharist was over time, taken away from them altogether. They no longer had any part in leadership. The only public task in mission which they retained was witnessing to the faith through service, practised especially in caring for the sick, visiting people in prison, and ministering to the needs of the poor and hungry. [17]

Women's roles in the mission of the church changed over the centuries, including for some who gave their lives as martyrs for their faith, such as Perpetua in the third century. Some became monastics, setting aside the role of wife and mother for a more ascetic life

---

[16] Lienemann-Perrin, C, 22
[17] Ibid, 25

as virgins, while others "set up their households as monastic sites including Macrina of Nyssa, Marcella, Paula and her daughters Blessila, Paulina and Eustochium and Rufina."[18]

In the seventh and eighth centuries women like Hugeberc of Hildesheim and Leoba left England to do mission work in Germany under Boniface. Hilda of Whitby ran an abbey for men and women and trained future male leaders in the church; she was connected to St Aidan and later St Cuthbert and their celtic style. This was part of the ministry of reawakening people in Northumberland, England to the gospel, and was supported by the community on Lindisfarne Island. Women like Hildegard of Bingen and Elizabeth of Schonau were twelfth-century mystics who brought the gift of prophetic vision to the church of its time, although they were greatly marginalised by the church hierarchy.

The history of the church's mission continued to show how women were limited in their ministries until the nineteenth century, when the modern mission movement began and women began to offer to serve overseas. According to Ruth Tucker, this movement of women in the late nineteenth and early twentieth centuries was the largest mass movement of women mobilised.

> The Women's Missionary Movement was born out of fervour for missions, but it was also born out of desperation- a desperation felt most keenly by single women called by God but rejected by men. Women had been denied opportunity to serve through traditional mission channels. They had served effectively as missionary wives and as fund-raisers and prayer warriors on the home front, but

---

[18] Dharmaraj, G. E., Women as border crossing agents: *Missiology* (1998) 26:1 58

they were not permitted to be missionaries in their own right.[19]

Through the success of such women's ventures, women were eventually accepted by mainstream organisations as missionaries. Women opened hospitals, trained nurses and doctors, cared for the handicapped, and became itinerant preachers. They ran bible colleges and trained pastors and church leaders in third-world countries. This proving ground for women led to changes from the mid-twentieth century to now, and to women being accepted by some mainline denominations as fully ordained leaders of the church. The first of these leaders had been former missionaries or deaconesses. Gender discrimination was not invented in our generation or century, but has been a dimension of the church's life and imperfect faith since its origins. Jesus's vision for the body of Christ to be counter-cultural had its challenges, and continues to be challenged as true gender equality has not yet been achieved.

Today in the twenty-first century, the church needs to continue accepting women who are called by God and allow them to serve in cooperation with men as equals in all areas of service, according to their gifts, graces, and calling. There are still some significant barriers to break through to enable women from every church background and culture to know the freedom of service and experience the grace of God and full acceptance as leaders, which Jesus Christ modelled for us. However, the mission of God, understood within this broader context of a relational God, could help convert the church as well as the world to a different way of being, living in the reign of God. Some of this challenge relates to the way in which we construct and understand leadership, which we come to in the next chapter.

---

[19] Tucker, R. A., Chapter 3 "Women in Mission" in Phillips, J. M, & Coote, R. T., *Toward the 21ˢᵗ Century in Christian Mission* (Michigan, 1993). 285

*"Life then is a contest............ or life then
is a community"* Deborah Tannen

CHAPTER 3

*Feminist perspectives on leadership
and Church leadership*

As we continue, let us ground the discussion of women in church leadership in the wider context of the literature on leadership and management in general society, in business, and in other institutions. I want to look at general understandings of leadership, and feminist reflections and perspectives of leadership in society generally. We will then focus on the experience of women in church leadership, and the challenges to live as servant leaders as valued equals with men for the building up of God's kingdom.

One of the burning issues in society over the last four decades has been defining what good or effective leadership looks like, and how it can be developed and channelled for good in the development of our society. Leadership's significance has risen in many sectors of society, including business, government, and the not-for-profit sector. The importance of leadership has become crucial in enabling people to work together to create a better world with material wealth whilst meeting human needs. This issue has been growing within this century, and its importance has become significant, yet there are no simple formulas. Leadership by definition is associated with the ability to inspire and motivate others to focus and follow a dream or vision. It implies that there must be followers for a leader to be truly effective within his or her sphere of influence.

Leadership is also being contrasted and compared with management and found to be a different force, which many businesses and organisations have been lacking. As much research has been done in business as to why some have been successful and others not, the importance of leadership and its quality and approach has been discovered clearly. Richard Higginson, in his work on transforming leadership, indicates that we have too much management and not enough leadership. Higginson makes this comparison on the basis of Bennis and Nanus's research on transformative leadership. This links leadership to a social ethic of justice, not often found in the secular business world. His assessment of that research states,

> Such leadership creates a common social responsibility. It engenders people who buy into a vision, know what needs doing and are happy to get on with it. Transformative leadership frees up and pools collective energies in pursuit of a common goal.[20]

In the past forty years since the rise of feminism in society, it has been noted by writers like Amanda Sinclair that leadership as understood by many in society is in fact constructed by males to maintain their own power and status in society. As women have challenged the roles that were set for them during the last forty years, many feminists concluded that leadership as we have known it is a male construct, which needs to be challenged rather than accepted. According to Sinclair,

---

[20] Higginson, R, "Second wave, third wave" in *Transforming leadership: A Christian approach to management* (London,1996) 26-27

Leadership is a social construction—the product of the emotional and often unconscious needs, early experiences and group aspirations of the led, as well as the traits and skills of the leader. Understanding these symbolic and mythic origins of leadership helps to explain our insatiable, and so often disappointed, hunger for leadership and why so few women are recognised as leaders. [21]

There has been some research done over the past twenty years on the role of women in leadership and indeed this research has also acknowledged that the way women lead, though different to men, is still leadership. Sinclair goes on to explore the differences gender can bring to leadership. She says,

Although there has been passing attention given to men leading women, it has been men in charge of other men that has captured the imagination of researchers and biographers and spawned their fascination for military and sporting exemplars. The twin tests of leadership have surely been the capacity of men to stand above other men. [22]

The fact that women leaders are not often held up as examples of good leadership highlights the bias that exists and the hierarchical way in which many males view leadership. There is often no comparison made about leadership styles. Being attuned to the feminist perspective where people bring their unique gifts can contribute to effective outcomes through a more collaborative style of leadership with and alongside the other. This is relevant

---

[21] Sinclair, A, *Doing Leadership Differently* (Melbourne,1998) 1

[22] Ibid, 15

in business, in society at large, and also within the church, where women model that style of leadership, yet that leadership is not recognised as equally valuable. Something as simple as how we perceive the function of conversations is very revealing in terms of gender difference. Deborah Tannen writes about the way in which men and women differ in how they see their place in the world and how they understand or misunderstand one another due to their frame of reference. In her study, she explains how this occurs in ordinary conversations. She writes,

> I now see that my husband was simply engaging in a way that most men do: as an individual in a hierarchical social order in which he was either one-up or one-down. In this world view, conversations are negotiations in which people try to achieve and maintain the upper hand if they can, and protect themselves from others' attempts to put them down, and push them around. Life then is a contest, a struggle to preserve independence and avoid failure. I on the other hand was approaching the world as many women do, as an individual in a network of connections. In this world, conversations are negotiations for closeness in which people try to seek and give confirmation and support, and to reach consensus. Life then is a community, a struggle to preserve intimacy and avoid isolation. [23]

It is no surprise then to discover that men and women working together in organisations may be unaware of the dynamics attached to the other, and are likely to be at cross purposes with each other.

---

[23] Tannen, D, *You just don't understand: Women and Men in conversation*, (New York, 2001) 24-25

The level of misunderstanding or confusion about social dynamics is very likely to inhibit clear direction and decision making, and make achieving goals and targets challenging. The challenge for women in organisations is to be able to bring their competencies to a male-dominated arena, wisely understanding the way decision making works, in order for their voices to be heard and their contributions taken seriously.

Feminism has unravelled and challenged the stereotype of male-dominated leadership. This kind of leadership is based on the belief that men are the dominant gender: they are the providers, they are smarter than women, and women who show them up must be kept in their place and not given power. The stereotypical male-dominated leadership has proven to be conservative, reactionary, and often unable to adapt to the demands of the twenty-first century. This unspoken sense of male entitlement is often the root cause of conflict and misunderstanding. Amanda Sinclair touches on this issue in her reflection on the nature of leadership today as being equally about relationships as well as function and purpose. She says, "leadership is a resource which resides in the group and must be cultivated in order for the group to fulfil its potential. Leadership is always a transaction not simply a function." [24] This implies that there are various parties who buy into it and make it work for its purpose or function.

Feminism and feminist theology within the church has helped uncover examples of how women lead differently. Feminism has enabled a reappraisal of the servant leadership model of Jesus Christ and his ministry by looking again at the biblical texts. Jesus's leadership was a transaction not a function. This has had a significant impact on the church, leading to a reinvestigation of the ministry of Jesus, a rediscovery of his empowerment of women and, through that, development of a model for Christian life and

---

[24] Sinclair, A, *Doing Leadership Differently* 34

ministry as service. It has validated people looking to discover Jesus's leadership style and how people can help build his kingdom by living out those values and attitudes with others in life. In Jesus, we saw the deep valuing of human life as God-given, and the purpose of ministry to bring good news, healing, and wholeness to people as individuals and communities.

This has a direct impact on how people are valued and treated in any social context, but specifically in the workplace. People are not human resources, but beings made in the image of God and made for a purpose to reveal and live out the grace of God in the world. Feminist theologian and retired Uniting Church Minister Rev Dr Dorothy McRae-McMahon says that, people are not things to be neatly calculated. They feel and can be depressed or inspired. They grieve and hope, sometimes like to care for each other, and don't necessarily work efficiently when stretched or stressed. [25]

This concept of servant leadership has been significant not only in the life of the church but in mainstream leadership and management training; much of that work has been done through the Harvard School of Business. A servant-leader focuses primarily on the growth and well-being of people and the communities to which they belong. While traditional leadership generally involves the accumulation and exercise of power by one at the top of the pyramid, servant leadership is different. The servant leader shares power, puts the needs of others first, and helps people develop and perform as highly as possible. According to Robert Greenleaf, the servant is leader not the leader is servant. He sees that servant leadership is not a quick-fix approach but something that has to be carefully developed within an institution with individuals and culture. He says,

---

[25] McRae-McMahon, D, *Daring Leadership for the 21st century* (Sydney, 2001) 72

> At its core, servant leadership is a long term, transformational approach to life and work-in essence, a way of being-that has the potential for creating positive change throughout our society. It deals with the reality of power in everyday life-its legitimacy, the ethical restraints upon it and the beneficial results that can be attained through the appropriate use of power. [26]

Leadership should be built on the foundation of relationship and followership rather than be purely functional. This is the challenge that feminism has brought to the long-held corporate views that women's leadership is not recognised as true or real leadership. This has led many women to lead in a man's style in order to gain recognition, otherwise their leadership is discounted or seen as inferior. Women are evaluated more negatively than men, even if they act the same way. This accounts for the lower levels of women in the higher levels of corporate life. The glass ceiling is still waiting to be smashed in many parts of society. In the church, even though some progress has been made, women's leadership still needs to be taken seriously and valued equally.

The issue of power and authority is a crucial one, and touches on one of the greatest threats to the acceptance of women in leadership, and particularly in the life of the church. Holding authority in a position of leadership is a great responsibility due to the influence for good or otherwise that flows from it. There are a variety of ways in which that is done, and these vary between genders and personalities. The unique way in which women see the place and role of authority is also interesting. Celia Hahn describes it this way.

---

[26] Greenleaf, R. K., *The Power of Servant Leadership* (San Francisco, 1998) 4-5

> Holding authority involves caring for people and purpose. Taking charge and leading courageously we want to engage with others in a mutual, collegial way. This is contrasted with much male leadership which is about power and directing people to do the tasks required with no significant register or concern for the person or the impact relationally at all. [27]

Carol Becker has written widely on women leaders in the church and has come to some practical insights into the changed roles of women, and the challenges of adaptation and sometimes compromise they face in order to find their way through the gender maze. She noted that women operate differently from men as leaders, and indeed have brought a new paradigm into being which has been met with huge opposition. The new paradigm is described in this way by her: "women encourage participation, share power and information, enhance other people's self-worth, and get others excited about their work."[28] Some of her other descriptions about women in leadership involve images of weaving and inclusion and emphasize the heart not the head—symbols of the ways that women lead differently.

The many traps that women can fall into in church leadership are numerous, and require wisdom, a strong sense of identity, and call by God to ministry leadership. Women have to claim the authority God has given to them as leaders, knowing that some may not accept them, some will struggle with them and experience great discomfort from their existence, while others will be richly supportive, loyal, and blessed through their ministry. As Celia Hahn rightly points out,

---

[27] Hahn, C. A., *Growing in authority: Relinquishing control* (Alban Institute, 1994) 4
[28] Becker, C. E., *Leading Women: How church women can avoid leadership traps and negotiate the gender maze* (Alban Institute, 2000) 52

> We in the church today are deeply concerned about
> how to live with authority; our understanding of it
> is fuzzy and contradictory; and we get little practical
> and personal help from those who talk about it
> in objective, institutional terms ... We need to
> become curious about our own inner experience of
> authority, probing our struggles and joys as people
> who exercise authority every day, and reclaiming the
> church's search for how the gospel story illuminates
> our inner and corporate life. [29]

There are challenges as women grow in their confidence and
are valued for their giftedness in the same way that they value other
people's giftedness in the life of the church. Many Christians have
moved away from hierarchical approaches to leadership to more
consultative, collaborative approaches, having been influenced by
feminist perspectives. Australian writers like Margot Cairnes and
Candy Tymson are examples of Australian women in business and
management circles who have brought their feminist understandings
and Catholic spirituality (which has a long tradition of the feminine
in theology), into mainstream leadership, management theory, and
practice. Margot Cairnes, a long-term writer about leadership for
Engineers Australia's journals and consultant to many top-listed
Australian companies, has written of changing the culture within
organisations in her book *Approaching the Corporate Heart*. She
has sought to implement more holistic strategies for leadership
development based on the servant leadership model.

Women generally come into ministry with a pastoral care focus,
a strong liturgical gifting, a strong connection to relational ministry,
a desire to build community through nurture, an awareness of
emotional needs, and a desire to take on the task of building a

---

[29] Hahn, C, 1994, 5

mission-focused community of faithful people. Men generally come with a more task-focused approach to ministry: to care for people but to lead through an organisational focus, to manage the structures, and work with what is present. Connecting back to Robert Greenleaf's work earlier, women tend to be the servant who is the leader, whereas men are generally conditioned to be the leader who is the servant. Men find it harder to operate as the servant who is the leader because of their own socialisation and patriarchal world views. These are deeply embedded within their identities, and demand a reworking of identity to lead in another way. This goes back to the call and how women and men see their call and gifts and roles to fulfil.

In the next chapter, we will review the history of women's ordination within the Uniting Church in Australia and my own journey being called to be ordained for ministry leadership.

..Ordination without discrimination on the grounds of gender is a fundamental implication of the gospel.

Social Responsibility and Justice Report-
Uniting Church in Australia 1990

CHAPTER 4

The role of women in Church leadership: a history of ordained ministry within the Uniting Church in Australia.

P rior to the formation of the Uniting Church in Australia (UCA) by church union in 1977, the three churches which came into Union had already accepted the ordination of women. The Congregational church ordained its first woman minister in 1926. Rev Winifred Kiek was ordained within the Congregational Union of South Australia. The Methodist Church was slower to move in that direction. In 1927 the President of the Victoria and Tasmania Methodist conference sought advice from the President-General of the Methodist Church. The President indicated that the Methodist book of laws stated that "candidates for ministry were based on the assumption that all candidates would be men". [30] Following a General Commission set up to investigate the matter in 1957, the General Methodist conference in 1966 decided it could

---

[30] Report of the Social Responsibility and Justice Commission of the Assembly Commission for Mission, March 1990 *"Why does the Uniting Church in Australia Ordain Women to the Ministry of the Word? 6*

see no barriers to women being ordained for ministry. Rev Margaret Sanders and Rev Coralie Ling were ordained in 1969.

The Presbyterian Church of Australia had concerns about women in leadership at this time as well, specifically regarding biblical authority and practicality in relation to the writings of St Paul on women and their roles in the early church. Under the work of Rev Alan Smart in 1962, various investigations were done and three reports were presented to the Presbyterian Synod. In his final report, he concluded that it was impossible to justify the continued exclusion of women from ministry leadership. Rev Molly Thalheimer was ordained in 1974.

In 1977, at the time of Union, there were thirty-six ordained women in ministry in the Uniting Church. By 1985, there were 101 women and 2323 ordained men; four percent of ordained ministers were women. They must have been amazing trailblazers, during a time of unparalleled social change and the rise of the women's liberation movement. In 1991, the first Aboriginal woman, Rev Liyapidiny Marika from Yirrkala, Arnhem Land, was ordained. Liyapidiny was forty-six, a widow, and mother of three children, and this was a historic moment. Whilst there was great rejoicing in these changing times when women were officially accepted into ministry leadership roles, by 1985 there were concerns that the Uniting Church was retreating from its earlier commitment to ensure that women could fully participate in all aspects of the church's life.

The 1985 Assembly established a task group to further research the status of women in the Uniting Church; it formed a Social Responsibility and Justice Committee in 1986 to look into issues of affirmative action, numbers of women in theological colleges, inclusive language in liturgy, and other women's issues. The Justice Committee recommended that the Uniting Church become an equal opportunity employer, which mobilised affirmative action for the inclusion of women in theological college faculties and required that at least a third of all church committees were to be comprised of women. It also recommended that there be proactive seeking of women for Synod and Assembly roles and that college syllabi include the works of women scholars. The colleges were tasked with encouraging students to accept women's ministry as equally valuable and not to block ordination where negative attitudes remained. These questions were asked as part of the candidate selection process in the colleges: Do you accept the equality of women and men in ministry? Do you accept the Uniting Church's view on infant baptism? There were many members and male candidates who were not fully supportive of the UCA's position on women as ministers at that time.

When the Social Responsibility and Justice Committee released its report 'Women in the Uniting Church in Australia' in 1988, there were great concerns raised by the lack of progress made. This mobilised women from across the nation. Many felt the report paid lip service to the issues facing women, but that there was no clear strategy for these issues to be addressed and resolved.

The UCA Yarra Valley Presbytery organised a National Conference for Women in Melbourne in 1990, and the response was so huge that not everyone could be accommodated. Women from all over Australia, both lay and ordained, gathered to discuss the 1988 report and resolved that the church could only be made whole when women considered themselves to be, and were, equals in the church. At this conference, recommendations and alterations were made to the 1988 report's findings and a strategy developed for implementation. As a result of this movement, a Commission for Women and Men was established within the Uniting Church in Australia.

The 1990 report, 'Why does the Uniting Church in Australia ordain women to the Ministry of the Word?', became the foundational document on the full acceptance of women as ordained people in ministry leadership, and it has been referred to over the church's recent history. The document states that we ordain both women and men to the Ministry of the Word because we believe ordination without discrimination on the grounds of gender is a fundamental implication of the gospel of God's love in Christ for all human beings, without exception.

Various issues were part of that reflection, including the idea that church tradition had its importance but there were times when the gospel called for change in some aspects of the church's life. In reflecting on the ministry of Jesus, his ministry with women, the inclusion of women as leaders in the early church and their more critical reading of the Pauline writings opposing women, the Commission determined that ordaining women was in full accordance with the gospel of Jesus Christ. In fact, the New Testament has very little to say about ordination of anyone, although some instruction was given about the appointment of presbyters and deacons. There was clear evidence of God's direction involving both women and men in leading and serving in those early years.

For 1990, that was radical in Australia, and led to other denominations being forced to consider their own positions on these matters as time went by and social attitudes changed. The road for the early ordained women was tough, as many had to fight for credibility and acceptance, and many churches were still unwilling to issue a call to women ministers. John Bodycomb, in an article about holy orders, described how the inclusion of women in ministry increased the levels of competency above what many men exercised. He said,

> It has become patently obvious that some of the women ordained in the past 12 years, (ie since Union) were far superior in competence to some men. In admitting women to the ministry, the Uniting Church has broken two millennia of male

monopoly on holy orders and in so doing, has made
a powerful statement about itself. In challenging
male domination, it has become a cultural leader
rather than being reactive to the culture of the
event. [31]

Women have brought the most publicly visible changes to
the Uniting Church in their leadership roles, through the non-
hierarchical styles of leadership they often embody. One of those
early trailblazers, Rev Dorothy McRae-McMahon, wrote in 1990,

> most women come freshly into decision making
> areas of the church from a woman culture which
> often has different forms of power. They are
> therefore better able to name the negative aspects
> of existing male dominated power structures. [32]

Since Church Union in 1977, women have been challenging
traditional sources of religious authority with respect to scripture
and tradition and expanding their understanding of religious life.
At that time, women were still victims of a male-dominated culture
that saw them as a threat. Since women have challenged the status
quo, it is not surprising that they have had to push hard to find
ministry positions. In the 1990s, women were stretching their wings
and seeking to carve out new pathways in ministry, but many of
them experienced significant backlash and opposition from people
of the baby boomer and builder generations. They carved the way
for people like me, who came into the ministry candidate selection
process during the early 1990s.

---

[31] Bodycomb, J, "Women in Holy Orders: the experiences of the Uniting Church".
Church Scene, 518, 28 July 1989. 56

[32] McRae-McMahon, D, "Power and authority in the Christian Church". Australian
Ministry, 2,4 Autumn 1990, 4

There are numerous instances of power plays by both male clergy and male lay leaders to keep women under control. This probably reflects the insecurity of some people in leadership roles, that they were fearful of their own vulnerabilities and unwilling to accept women as equals.

There were many battles to be fought and one step at time was needed to keep trusting God's call, knowing that change would continue to be possible. Through the power of the Holy Spirit and through much perseverance and wisdom, the support of the sisterhood made these women strong and determined to bring lasting change. John Bodycomb's research back in 1989 and the following years named the challenges like this:

> Difficulties that have existed since church union include women being treated patronisingly or paternalistically by their male counterparts because the social conditioning of some males makes it difficult to deal with women who are demonstrably equal or better than they are. [33]

Women have been, and are still, in the minority in terms of percentage of women ordained. In the 2016 National Church Life Survey (NCLS) results within the Uniting Church in Australia NSW/ACT showed, 32 percent of ordained ministers were women. The percentage has changed from 4 percent in 1985 to 32 percent in 2016 to 24 percent in 2021. I thought that by now, at least 50 percent of ministers would be women, knowing the doorways were open for them and seeing what amazing work they have done in the Uniting Church. After forty years of the ordination of women, the percentages hadn't grown as much as I had expected. I think the decline in numbers is a reflection of the difficult treatment some

---

[33] Bodycomb, J, 6

women ministers have experienced, which has led them to leave or not to fulfil that call because they are unwilling to be treated badly. Many women have moved into lay leadership roles like the UCA specified ministry of Pastor, which does not challenge the power structures of the church in the same way as ordination does. I could certainly write a book about my personal experiences of negative treatment over the past twenty-five years, being an ordained woman minister in the Uniting Church since 1997, but perhaps that's the subject of another book at another time.

I am proud of what the Uniting Church has achieved in having the courage, since 1977 and later in 1990, to open the way for the gifts of called men and women to be formed into Ministers of the gospel. In spite of the tough journey that this has been for some of them, the fact that women continue to hold significant leadership roles throughout all the councils of the Uniting Church is a blessing for the world in which we live and the people that we serve.

Many other denominations in Australia have sought to bring about change and allow women to be priests or deacons. Many of the larger charismatic churches have women who are pastors, although that is often tied to being part of a married couple serving together. Many Anglican dioceses around Australia train and ordain women as deacons and priests, and so further ministry leadership opportunities continue to be made available to women God calls to serve and lead.

My own journey was from an Anglican background where women could not be ordained, except as deaconesses. After exploring cross-cultural mission work in the early 1980s and what my call might be, and having been a trained primary school educator, I discovered the Uniting Church accepted women for ordination. After a failed attempt to be taken seriously as a lay preacher within the Anglican church that I attended for years, and after moving to a local Uniting Church when newly married, I applied to become a lay preacher in the Uniting Church. This was accepted with openness and further study began for me, along with opportunities to adapt to the way the consensus-based Uniting Church worked.

In the early 1990s, I studied part time at United Theological College, and even with a young child, I was warmly accepted into the student body. Within three years, I felt that my call to ministry needed to be tested. I wondered whether becoming a Minister of the Word was God's leading for me. It took me some time to realise that it was okay to be a woman and have this call to ministry, that I would be taken seriously, and that God was not putting up barriers. The Uniting Church was open for me to discover my life's call, and I had a husband who encouraged me along the way and has supported me ever since.

In 1993, I was accepted as a candidate for ministry and continued study to fulfil all academic and formational requirements. During that formation time, I was blessed to be mentored by Rev Norma Brown and Rev Margaret Joyce, to work with Rev Diane Anderson (*née* Stanton) in field education placement, and other women I met through theological college and wider church, including Rev Dr Rhonda White and Rev Maz Smith.

In Chapter 5, I will share some of the experiences of these earlier women ministers mentioned here during the 1980s and 1990s as I began the next phase of my journey in ministry.

Know your gifts and strengths and make your placements according to your gifts.
Wise woman Minister

CHAPTER 5

*The experience of ordained women ministers
in the Uniting Church (1980-1995)*

I was deeply inspired by other women who had been ordained for ministry in the late 1980s and early 1990s during my formation time at United Theological College, North Parramatta. While enrolled in the course Uniting Church Studies in 1994, I endeavoured to discover something of their early experiences in ministry by doing some practical interviewing and research. Whilst some of this was done through a written survey to a larger group, the greatest gift was holding intentional conversations with five women as part of an oral history of their experience.

The survey had questions that related to call, theological training, joys, difficulties, and useful qualities needed for ministry leadership. The key issues that seemed consistent were in relation to the unique contributions they made in ministry, the strengths needed for longevity given the overt sexism some faced, and the cultural factors that the church needed to put in place in order to sustain them. Of these five women, all five were married and had children of varying ages, from infants to adults. Four were in parish/congregation ministry and one was in chaplaincy.

These women had positive experiences of their theological training, which provided deep understanding of the Christian faith, dealt with the diversity of theologies which had emerged in the 1970s through the 1990s, and gave a firm foundation upon which to develop their ministry. In addition, it helped to expand their understanding of God and who they were in relation to God. The feminist perspective had been a help in affirming women in their calling, reshaping the focus of their ministry, and giving them a stronger sense of identity in God.

Their responses included the joys of seeing people come to faith, growing in grace, and sharing the love of God with others in their communities. There were also the joys of building Christian community and the challenges of building new congregations, which meant rethinking the conventional ways in which the church operated and creating new models or ways ahead. Most women also believed they were able to present a fresh and different face of the church to people in the wider community and society. This was generally accepted in a positive light. Some people's perceptions were that it was good the church was changing in line with society and that it might become more relevant and more connected to the issues people really faced in daily life.

There was still a tremendous amount of sexism present within the church at that time. Despite the fact that women had been ordained in the Uniting Church since 1977, seventeen years later attitudes had been slow to change. There was still suspicion in many parts of the church about letting women have equal status and power. The perception that women may not be up to the task still prevailed, despite the fact that many wonderful women had proved their worth over many years, and in some cases, were recognized as more competent. Some of this related to the perceptions of the way women use power and exert authority. There seemed to be great discomfort or lack of understanding of different leadership styles and of the idea that there could be a variety of ways in which people could exercise leadership in the church, including in team ministries.

Some male ministers lacked confidence in how they might relate to women ministers as colleagues in equal standing. They were not to be dominated or made subservient but were equals. Discomfort at being shown up by the competence of some women ministers already in placements, and having to find new ways of relating to them as equals was an understandable threat to the security of some male ministers. This issue would have to be tackled in the Uniting Church more thoroughly as more women entered the ministry, working towards ordination and full pastoral leadership.

The notion of doing theology from a minority perspective rather than a majority perspective was also something that women were used to. These women ministers knew what it was like to be marginalized in the church, as the church had continued to be marginalized in society since the 1990s. It meant that women ministers had some skills of resilience to meet the challenges which had come to them, as they were accustomed to being adaptable and flexible from being marginalized in the past.

One of the joys these women mentioned was that other people, particularly women, began to see themselves differently, because women ministers had given them permission to think more broadly. One comment was that some women didn't think they were made in the image of God, and that only men were made in the image of God. Since traditionally God had been imaged as Father and male, some women perceived themselves as inferior. This opened up people's insights into Christianity, that it was not a religion focused on people being in or out due to right belief, but about grace and inclusion.

The interviewees found that there were barriers to their acceptance as equals with male ministers, particularly if they were mothers of younger dependent children, and some experienced some unfair treatment. Some people in churches argued that these ministers would not be accessible enough in the parish when they were needed, and thus availability of settlements/placements was more difficult and restricted for them. Others found that their parishes were blessed to have a woman who could be more flexible in her time management.

Another area of difference for women was that they were seen as more relationship-oriented than task-oriented in their pastoral ministry. This could be seen as a weakness in women ministers because the church had inherited the male minister model of the lone ranger type. The expectation that ministers should work seventy to eighty hours per week, and that their spouses would also do their share of church work, was commonplace in the 1990s. It has taken over thirty years to dispel the myth that you get two for the price of one, and some churches still have unrealistic expectations of both spouses. It is interesting that women Ministers with husbands find their husbands are not expected to take on leadership roles in the church, and yet in spite of most male ministers' female spouses working full time, there is still some sense of expectation that they would give time and involvement to the church. Such is the double standard both ways to the disadvantage of women.

Some of the advantages that these pioneering women found were that many people in churches gave themselves permission to show their feelings more openly. This was an advantage with other women but sometimes harder when visiting men. It was also more effective in a chaplaincy role where women were more widely accepted in caring, nurturing roles than men. On the other hand, in working with some Culturally and Linguistically Diverse (CALD) congregations, women were not easily accepted as ministry leaders although some male colleagues may have referred other women to the woman minister for cultural reasons. All of these women were from an Anglo-Celtic background, although they shared churches where people and ministers from CALD backgrounds held services and shared properties. This created some interesting dynamics in the 1990s, but as relationships formed and professional acceptance was gained, some very positive cross-cultural opportunities emerged. This has changed significantly over the past thirty years, and many women from CALD backgrounds have moved into formation for ordained ministry leadership; in addition, attitudes are changing for fuller acceptance of women ministers in Anglo-Celtic, multicultural, and mono-ethnic congregational settings.

Another of the challenges was that younger women ministers found people were unsure about how to work with the power and authority they held as pastoral and missional leaders of the church. Some tried to protect them, as in a familial parent-child dynamic, while others found they were patronized or treated harshly because their power or position in the church was a threat to the position some male lay leaders held. The older the woman, the less difficult an issue it was for these women ministers. They also indicated that as wives and mothers, who have learned to be disciplined and good time managers, they have an advantage as ministry is very demanding and multi-faceted. Women also have a more circular understanding of life, of relationships, and of being connected with people, compared with men, who are generally more task oriented. Some older women who had matriarchal power within congregations were also threatened by women ministers, especially those who came as change agents.

In conclusion, the qualities these trailblazing ordained women believed future women would be required to have, in order to sustain an effective ministry, included the need to:

- have a thick skin, don't take yourself too seriously, and learn to pick your fights;
- be certain of your call from God and a vision for the type of ministry you want to exercise as placements will be harder to obtain;
- learn how to work within the highly political, consensus-based system that Uniting Church has developed, as men will use the system more effectively than women;
- be open to the collaborative, collegial relationships and support which other women in ministry can provide one another;
- trust yourself, have confidence in your calling, and claim the uniqueness of the different way you will offer ministry leadership;
- don't fall into the trap of thinking you have to be better than a man;
- know your gifts and strengths, make your placements according to your gifts, and don't be too nice about trying to do everything;
- have a deep joy based on your faith in Christ and valuing people and learning to be, instead of getting caught up in constant activity; and
- be independent and interdependent, flexible, humble in decision making, and courageous in being different.

At the end of each week, all you can say is that you have done your best and the rest is up to God. After all, God will make it what it needs to be. The identity which a woman minister has developed of herself will play an integral part in her being accepted and in championing the cause of equality between the genders. My observation is that women have had to struggle more deeply with the issue of who they are in relation to God and to the church. It is the certainty of that knowledge which enables them to continue to serve, even under a variety of tremendous pressures. In the next chapter, I will focus on my early experiences of being an ordained minister from 1997.

If you thought college was challenging, wait until you get your first parish! Me

CHAPTER 6

My early years of ministry leadership in the Uniting Church (1997-2003)

I was deeply grateful to the women I worked with during my formation and training time, who served as my field educators and mentors. They gave me helpful, grounded role models to reflect with about what this new ministry journey might be like. Getting a first placement was difficult not only because some congregations were still coming to terms with whether they would be comfortable having an ordained woman as their minister, but also because of my husband's employment commitments in Sydney. I was open to working part time or full time but the first placement didn't arrive until a full year after college finished. That was challenging in a number of ways, as most of my colleagues moved into their placements early the following year. In hindsight, it was God making me wait for the right place to become vacant. It also gave me time to do some supply ministry; that meant my first baptisms and first funerals, and my worship-leading skills were honed, without the full load of administration and property responsibilities.

There was real excitement in November 1997 when, after ordination, I began working in my first parish in western Sydney as a Uniting Church minister. As the first woman minister the parish had called, with two congregations in one parish to work with, I began a long and multi-faceted journey of missional leadership and service. Being the mother of a young school-aged child was an advantage when it came to developing ministry to families, as the local school was nearby and it became part of the network of people to connect with for the church's mission. I was well accepted by families in the local community as well as the congregational members of all ages, many from CALD backgrounds.

Supporting ministry to families through a long day care centre, supporting the after-school literacy centre, and conducting special worship events for all generations was the focus of my work in one congregation, and trying to build engagement with the local community with the other congregation. Some of the focus was on building up people's faith and community links between them, as well as discipleship growth and leadership development. Planning and leading several Alpha courses and later the Network course from Willow Creek Church in the United States were key growing points of personal faith and community building within both these churches.

I found great satisfaction in engaging with a congregation who wanted to be in mission, were willing to try new things, and were committed to improving their facilities in order to enhance the programmes and activities they already provided to the community. Generally, my leadership was well accepted within the congregations and in the wider community. I began in this role part time, so setting clear boundaries was essential, and ensuring that days off were maintained and family time guarded was important. Refocusing the congregation's priorities for mission was my priority and passion, so bringing about change through new ventures and well-developed and owned mission plans was essential. Being a change agent in the late 1990s was necessary for leaders if the church was to have any future relevance and impact in the lives of people moving into a new millennium.

One of the ways in which the church grew in its depth of community was through my introduction to them of the Alpha course from the United Kingdom. Whilst it had often been framed as an evangelistic programme that meets people with their questions of the faith, it had tremendous power to build the relationships of people within the church community. People who had been members together of the church for decades met, ate, watched video talks, and shared their experience of Christ with one another. So many of them said it had revolutionised their lives, because they understood their faith better, and it brought them closer to God and to one another. The depth of understanding and care for one another grew and motivated many to step up and serve, finding ways they could share with others what Jesus meant to them. This was exciting and a privilege to be part of, to witness people's blossoming and growth. It brought the church alive in a new way that helped motivate its mission, not to ensure the survival of the church but to share the love of God more naturally, which gave them joy.

One of the traps I fell into early was in trying to prove myself as a good minister. Being under forty with a school aged child but with great ambition to serve God and the church faithfully, I worked very hard. I felt that I had to prove I was not just as good as a male minister but better. This journey became very exhausting, and regular supervision and collegial relationships with other women enabled me to find and maintain a better balance. Strange advice from an elder at the time, but something that I have continued to realise and pass on to other colleagues is this: 'the more you do, the more people expect you to do! So be careful how much you do.'

We can set ourselves up for burn-out without having the necessary self-care, time out, and more realistic expectations of the workload to be carried and the impact it can have on us. This was good advice and allowed me to be clearer about not pleasing everyone and not setting myself up for failure and burn-out. Strong and positive pastoral care ministry was very taxing, but enabled me to be with people in the most privileged times in their lives, and much grace was shared and blessing received in that service.

One highlight for me was participating in a service for the Week of Prayer for Christian Unity, organised by the local Catholic priest with the Anglican and Baptist minister and held at the Catholic church. Ecumenically in that area, there was no ministers' network or ministers' fraternal, and none of the other denominations were supportive of having ordained women ministers. However, this was quite a breakthrough opportunity, and the Catholic priest came the following year to the Uniting Church for the service when we hosted it. These may seem trivial, but it seems that as people build relationships of trust across theological or ecclesiological divides, men's and women's attitudes can change and ideologies soften as we discover our common calling in Christ's service.

I enjoyed the liturgical role for both congregations and getting to know the people in both centres, who were nearby geographically. They were like chalk and cheese in relation to their understanding of church and practice of mission. This made the first year very interesting as it became clear early on that the parish was not a healthy structure to enable each congregation to grow its mission and share its resources fairly. As new regulations from the Assembly to remove the requirement that congregations be part of a parish structure had come into effect, the parish, in consultation with the Presbytery, decided to restructure and become two linked congregations. This was due to significant conflict between the leadership of each congregation that hampered their ability to enact their mission plans. This meant that the parish was split into two linked congregations; each would have its own church council, equally share ministry costs, and could move forward without conflict.

My first year was quite challenging, identifying the issues and working with both congregations to move into a new structured arrangement. In those days, parish councils were the core administrative decision-making body, along with elders' councils. This meant creating two new church councils and multiple committees for pastoral care and property matters. This work was brought to completion in February 1999, when the parish became one of the first parishes to become two linked congregations with their own church councils, no longer bound together. This was challenging but enabled each congregation to find its voice and focus its energy on mission for the future. The disadvantage for me was double church council meetings, property committees, elders' meetings, and other mission task groups. It did, however, set them up for greater success in their mission, if they were willing to step out in faith.

Overall, my first placement was really two different placements, as I moved on from one congregation after three years and focused on growing the mission with the other for an additional three years. These were filled with many joys and much growth, stronger cross-cultural ministry within the family ministry, and the addition of a second staff person whose focus was on family ministry. The church was larger and stronger when I moved on in 2003, and building up the leadership resources and being flexible about worship music and styles of service was important in creating variety and in setting them up for a positive future.

One of the most challenging aspects of leadership during this period was learning how to use the power and authority placed on me by God and the Church within the decision making and power structures of the local church. These would be the most painful experiences of ministry and learning. My experience was that the older lay male leaders were the most difficult people to work with, due to my claiming my ministerial power and authority with them. This was seen as a threat to their positional power, and became a source of conflict, especially since I was a younger woman minister. This is where knowing who we are in God and guarding against our own ego needs but keeping things in perspective is so important. The advice from those earlier women who said 'learn to pick your fights, and have a thick skin' was not always easy to implement. Sometimes standing your ground and ensuring that your spiritual resources are strongly in place are what you can do. Also, some of the older people did not like change and resisted it strongly. The challenge of being a female change agent was often doubly painful due to the intensity of the bullying behaviour or withdrawal of support that occurred.

I was very fortunate to have a working husband who was willing and able to support me in multiple ways, including negotiating a part-time role for himself initially for the first three years of my placement. He was and still is an amazing support, always acknowledged the call God gave me, and faithfully supported that as part of his own discipleship journey. He later resumed full-time work, taking a fair load of parental responsibilities during those early years and into the high school years too. He also has continued to be an advocate for women in leadership within the construction and engineering industry, and been a champion for change not only within his own company but in wider circles within Roads Australia and Consult Australia roundtables.

My next move was into a resourcing role in a presbytery/diocese, which provided the freedom to work across a variety of church settings, spread my wings, and bring what I had learnt into another part of the Uniting Church.

The joy of seeing churches wanting to move forward and doing new things. Me

CHAPTER 7

*Changing face of mission and leadership
in the early 2000s (2003-2011)*

The next exciting chapter in my ministry journey was in working directly for a group of churches in a region, called a presbytery in the Uniting Church, in the role of Mission Development Consultant for five years. This took me from one side of Sydney to the other and was a huge culture shock. I moved from the working-class western suburbs of Sydney to the lower north shore, a more affluent region, and this was very dislocating for a while. This was not a choice I would have deliberately made, moving to a wealthier area, but it was the call to serve in a resourcing role across a region that excited me. It would enable me to draw on all my teaching, mission, and ministry experience from the previous six years.

By 2003, there were more women in active ministry, and within this region greater acceptance of women leading local churches than I had expected. The presbytery had a greater emphasis on growing strong leaders for change and mentoring people into these roles in the wider church. There was also a growing awareness that churches were not growing and change was needed. I came into this work at a time when strategic planning for local churches and presbyteries was being actively developed and encouraged across the state. I was able to influence plans and processes within the presbytery, develop resources for consultation work, encourage new ventures, and support people leading them.

During this time, I was able to undertake further study in church leadership, management, missiology and supervision within a Master of Ministry programme. This included the development of a new mission initiative amongst business people in the North Sydney Central Business District as part of a research project assignment. I also became involved in the formation programme of the theological college and provided supervision for the occasional candidate for ministry during his or her field education programme. There were more women continuing to come into ministry training and more placements becoming open to ordained women. This work was very fulfilling; I worked alongside a variety of ministers and congregations, and sought to grow new mission and connect effectively with their local communities. I did this through building solid, trusting relationships with key leaders and groups within different congregations, pointed them to resources that could assist them, developed mission plans with them, and generally sought to build up a positive, hopeful, and prayerful approach.

Part of the work as Mission Development Consultant involved consulting with churches about their strengths and weaknesses, seeking to develop clearer vision and planning for the future, and reflecting on the overall life and witness of the congregation in its community. There was also work on assessment of the resources that different congregations held and how they could be better utilised for the strengthening of worship, witness, and service, including property redevelopments. One of the advantages I had in this work was my ability to be flexible, to respond to a variety of different contexts, and deal with various different issues in parallel. I loved this type of work, working alongside others and enabling many different new ventures to take off, giving support, and expediting decisions through the presbytery committee structure. I sought to support a permission-giving structure. I was privileged to see the plans of congregations become realities with new groups, new buildings, and new forms of church emerging during this time. Being a woman minister among other women was a great experience, although there were times when I missed the sense of belonging to a particular faith community in a liturgical role. Eco theology was on the rise and various projects and initiatives were begun which I was able to support and cultivate.

Part of my role involved becoming part of the oversight of new mission initiatives as a member of the Board of Mission overseeing state-wide initiatives. This was a wider picture, again, of the whole state and included much diversity in terms of rural and urban ministry, as well as new ways to structure ministry leadership within these changed circumstances. I enjoyed the challenge of connecting with people's plans and vision for mission in different places, rural and urban, with young and old. I also became part of the Synod Mission Resource Fund committee for several years, which involved having oversight of special funding that had been provided to support new and existing fresh expressions of mission and outreach. This was a creative space, and being on the cutting edge of new initiatives and enabling resources to be made available for new ventures was incredibly satisfying. Being a woman in ministry in this context was easier than working in a congregational setting. There was room to be creative, to take initiative, and to pastorally support people who were trailblazing new ways to connect with the community and support these projects to grow and be sustainable in the longer term. It allowed me to work within the structures and to achieve some positive outcomes with and for congregations. Here as a woman minister, I was well accepted.

Whilst there were administrative aspects to this work, I grew in my connection to wider church bodies and systems and thought more about how our church system worked. In this space, the idealist came out in me, and whilst I sought to bring about cultural change within the presbytery system, my challenges were not easily received. I was also aware that when ethical issues involving the ministry practice of colleagues arose, it was difficult to bring about a just resolution after calling out behaviour that other people don't want to deal with. As an insightful minister with a strong radar for noticing boundary-crossing behaviour, I experienced ongoing backlash and subtle verbal attacks for daring to challenge a male minister's behaviour. I felt betrayed by some ministry colleagues, with whom I had worked closely. It was like the boys' club all ganged up against me, and it was very painful. My insights were well founded and the person was later removed from ministry, but I felt betrayed by some whom I had respected highly. I wondered if this was the cost of being a woman minister willing to uphold the standards of the code of ethics and ministry practice.

Men still held the overall power in that system, and did not want to deal with it directly, so they treated me badly. We have complaints processes but when others don't want to face speaking the truth to keep the church a safe place, some painful outcomes can result. How can women bring about lasting change when men still dominate the power structures? My work on the state-wide Synod's Discipline Committee for ten years reinforced that view; however, being a woman in that space was very important, as your voice is clearly heard, your perspective is highly valued, and ethical breaches were followed by just outcomes

I've often thought about the fact that I had to let go of that wider role when I could have stayed there and been more of a change agent. The timing and funding around that work was ending and I knew that a person who would maintain the status quo was preferred over me, as I would have continued to try to bring about cultural changes within the organisation and improve the gender balance. It is always hard to do these types of roles when you are the only woman in the room. There is always the default setting of how things have been done in the past or how much time and effort people are willing to give to bring significant change.

Most of my congregation placements were on a part-time basis, originally due to the younger age of my daughter and wanting to have some quality parenting time. I was willing to go into placements where there was potential for growth, in both mission and in financial resources.

One of the observations I'd make about women in ministry is that having been used to being flexible as women and sometimes mothers, having moved and morphed into different contexts, many women move in and out of various types of placements very successfully. I loved the diversity and challenge of this ministry setting, but eventually wanted to move forward into another congregation and new mission setting, seeking to implement new ideas and ways of doing ministry which I'd been doing with others. This opened up in mid-2008 when I moved to the south west of Sydney into a congregation and church plant ministry. We build the reign of God not our own kingdoms, and there is no straightforward or clear career path or progression in ministry settings. Much can change with funding, changes to structures, wider church vision, and mission strategy. People in systems have to be flexible or they can become obsolete very quickly.

In the UCA, professional supervision for people in ministry has been mandated since 1997 as part of adherence to the Code of Ethics and Ministry Practice for all ordained people. Since I had received good supervision on my ministry during these years, and was openly encouraged to train as a supervisor given my good pastoral skills and reflective ability, I began training as a professional supervisor in 2008. This became part of my calling too. From 2008 to 2010, I upskilled myself to become a Professional Supervisor, through a supervisory training course with Transforming Practices Inc, an independent pastoral supervision association and community of practice. I enjoyed the freedom to develop my supervision practice and was sought out by many in those early years, including, surprisingly, a number of male ministers from CALD backgrounds.

Those first fourteen years of ministry were growing and positive years for women in ministry leadership, although some backward movement occurred; quotas for a minimum of one third female membership on committees began to be wound back. By this time, there had been some backlash against women in ministry in the wider Church. Many were experiencing, as I had, not being taken seriously, being treated with disrespect, and needing to seek out the support of other women in ministry through organising networks of care for one another. A number of times during those years, I started women ministers' dinners or lunches to get women together in a debriefing space and for some fun and collegiality. This kept our spirits up and reminded us that we were not alone in this journey and that God was providing companions on the road.

The Uniting Church NSW/ACT Synod had some significant financial problems in these years, and had heavily funded all presbyteries for mission consulting work and new growth. Once that money dried up, it became clear that the current system was unsustainable. By the end of 2011, having been involved in a task group affecting the restructuring and amalgamation of the work of the Mission and Education boards into one, which involved a large number of forced redundancies, I took time out from congregational ministry placements for three years. I developed a private practice in professional and pastoral supervision, which provided a new form of ministry for me to exercise. I supported others in reflection on their ministries and included people from other denominations in that reflection. This continues through to this day. I also became a trainer of professional and pastoral supervisors in 2016.

*Everything you want to know about current
women minister's experience and have decided to
ask! Get ready for the honest answers! Me*

CHAPTER 8

*The experiences of current women
ministers serving today (2011-2021)*

Much progress has been made and there is more to be done to enable people within the church to embrace the giftedness of women in leadership, and for the Church to lead the way for society. To bring wholeness to people's lives, and to experience the fullness of Christ's love and grace through those who God called to serve as leaders in this millennium, is an important way ahead. There are many options to be considered for women in the face of overt or tacit opposition or subversion. There are also challenges in the current #MeToo era, in which there has been an erosion of respect for women generally, in ordained leadership roles, and a backlash which has had a negative impact on some women being willing to move into higher level leadership roles within presbyteries, synods, or boards. Having talked about the glass ceiling in higher level management and leadership roles in business and church organisations earlier, one might have to say that smashing through a glass ceiling is likely to be quite painful, cause hurt or harm, and may not be worth all the effort to simply get to where women should be.

My experience of ministry in the 2010's was one where I experienced that backlash, especially with the loss of minimum quotas of at least one third women on all boards and committees. Being the only woman in the room often felt risky, and sometimes led to negative or dismissive comments, not being given credit for work that had been done, or being minimised by male presbytery leaders. Sometimes women chose to move out of the system because they couldn't find the level of respect they deserved, found it painful to have to justify their existence, and felt the value of their contribution was minimised. Their leadership was not seen as strong or assertive, because it was more relational and collaborative. Some women got tired of not being understood or valued for the different perspectives they could bring, which was God's gift for the church but was sometimes ignored.

Because of such experiences, I opted out of the system for a few years after I became trained as a professional supervisor. I found much freedom in being my own boss and having immense freedom to draw on all my ministry experience as I journeyed alongside others as they reflected on their ministry experience. This highlights just how progressive the Uniting Church is, with many denominations still not open to ordaining women priests, ministers, or pastors in the Church in 2021 but willing to accept us as supervisors.

I have been reflecting on the fact that there has been some decline in the numbers of women who are still in active ministry within the UCA. The survey of current women ministers of the Uniting Church in NSW/ACT, which I undertook at the beginning of 2021, has been very revealing. The fact that we still exist and are still offering strong, pastoral, and effective leadership in a multitude of places is a gift to the church and the kingdom of God, in spite of efforts to minimise or cause us harm. It may reflect the wider backlash in society against women in leadership generally, as we had with the harsh treatment of the first woman prime minister of

Australia, Ms Julia Gillard. It may reflect the backlash against the #MeToo movement, where women stood up and spoke out about ill treatment, sexual violence, and ostracism for whistle blowing against paedophiles and calling out unethical, sexist behaviour. Church systems have been rocked by their failure to deal justly with child victims of sexual abuse, as well as other community organisations which failed to protect children and discipline and prosecute offenders in their ranks.

So what were the responses that current Uniting Church women ministers within NSW/ACT have made about their present experience? This will be the focus of this chapter. The survey was set up electronically and anonymously, with a link sent to fifty women ministers currently in active ministry. The survey involved ten questions, some of which gave clear choices and others where free responses were possible. Two thirds of these ministers were working in local church settings in parishes or congregations while the other third was spread out amongst chaplaincy, presbytery or synod roles. 32 percent had been in ministry from one to ten years, 27 percent had been in ministry for ten to twenty years, and 41 percent had been in ministry for more than twenty years. 90 percent had experienced times of challenge related to their gender (see survey in Appendix 1).

When asked about the nature of these challenges, some of the responses were quite shocking. Many responses indicated that in working ecumenically, many male ministers and members from other denominations ignored them, treated them in a patronising way, and challenged their right to be in a church leadership role at all. This was particularly so in ministers' associations with more conservative denominations. Many felt that others didn't take them seriously, that their ordinations were not recognised or seen as equal with men, and that they were not seen as real ministers or as doing the children's and women's work only. Others spoke about the lack of acceptance from within the UCA, particularly in rural congregations, where they said the men supported women in ministry but messed them around, and patronised and dominated them on committees. Some expressed concern about being shut out of decision making by other male leaders who put them down, saying things like, 'God had to call you because the men were not listening!' Some spoke of harassment and inappropriate comments about their clothing, appearance, and prettiness from male colleagues or church members. Some felt they weren't taken seriously as professionals, or that only their pastoral skills were valued, but not their preaching and leadership skills in church councils and in administration. Some spoke of being bullied and feeling that they still had to prove themselves as worthy of being leaders, even though men did not have to prove themselves.

Some women who had clergy husbands expressed times when their husbands were given credit for their ideas or work by other people rather than themselves, and people introduced them as Rev X's wife rather than as Rev Y in her own right. Some women found that their competence was questioned or their priorities challenged if they had younger children. Some church women even questioned whether they could be good mothers and wives as well as good ministers. There were also challenges in working within different cultures which are generally more patriarchal. This was sad to hear, as it sounded so similar to what I heard from my original survey back in 1994, before I was ordained and moved into ministry. Those views were expressed by women ministers in the earlier years of ordained ministry, when women ministers were still seen as a novelty. I thought that things would have improved much more over the past twenty-five years than has been the case.

The follow up to that question was asking these women to identify the strategies they used to overcome or gain support to effectively resolve them. This was very interesting as there was a wide range of strategies named. Many found that the support of other women colleagues provided great strength, knowing that others had also been through similar experiences and shared their ideas. Others claimed their strength from biblical stories that empowered them to stand their ground, sometimes to call out bad behaviour and to ensure they have been heard. Some sought to find the good, to get on with the job of ministry and not see gender issues behind every challenge. While others reflected that they have realised the challenges are more related to their style of ministry than gender, being a change agent, truth teller, and confronter of deep issues will always be a challenge, regardless of gender.

Some women found wearing a clergy collar gave them more visibility and enabled them to be more assertive and to jump into conversations; if spoken over by a man, they would say 'I haven't finished what I was trying to say if you would let me finish' or 'I don't think you quite understand what I was saying.' Others found ways in ecumenical situations of working consultatively and inclusively, speaking when they really had something they wanted to say, and building trusting relationships with colleagues. Some tried to deal with the challenges by asking questions about why things are difficult, wondering why things happen, to open people up to reflect. Others were very hurt by their experience and felt lack of support from presbyteries; some had to leave placements or made formal complaints. Many women said they still felt they had to work harder to be respected and so they worked harder. One of the respondents brought some humour into the space, saying, 'If you have an issue with women in ministry then you better take it up with God as God is the one who has not only called me, but given me gifts for this leadership.' Generally, one of the strategies for working on solutions was to provide some education around these issues. Men with insight need to be made aware that they can help be part of the solution and remove some of the blindness that still exists about excluding others or not respecting differences.

Alongside these challenges, there were many joys which women ministers experienced. Many of these revolved around the joy of leading worship, walking with people in faith as they grow, helping people discover their dreams for serving God, the blessing of the people in the church and their faithfulness to God, and embracing change. Other joys included teaching, leading change within the church and building good teams for leadership, and working with organisations beyond the church. People witnessed the healing of others, people beyond the local church who became open to spirituality because these women presented a different image or view of God or a minister than the stereotype. Many were energised by leading and coaching people in mission and seeing real impact in transforming their local communities into safe, inclusive faith communities. I can't say whether the joys outweighed the challenges, but these women were dedicated to living out their ordination vows and call by God and were sustained by Christ.

In asking about the spiritual resources that enabled them to develop resilience, 95 percent pointed to professional supervision and strong collegial relationships with other women as the resources that most sustained them. 72 percent indicated prayer as the next most important resource followed by Bible reading (63 percent), retreats and study (54 percent), journaling (36 percent), and other resources not specified (31 percent). This was an interesting finding, given that I moved into professional supervision in 2008 partly because my own experience of ministry had been tough. I probably would have given up during my first placement without the support of a good supervisor. Good supervision enabled me to build up my skills and resources and integrate myself, faith, identity, and call to become more resilient and continue on in ministry. Twenty-five years later and I'm still here, thanks be to God and thanks to many amazing colleagues who have been part of that journey!

This has been a short summary of the experiences of some current women ministers. The next chapter will focus on the areas these women have identified where change is needed to enable a more respectful church community for women leaders and qualities they identified that future women leaders will need to have to survive and thrive.

*How can we bring about change that makes
a more inclusive church for
women Ministers of the present and future? Me*

CHAPTER 9

Changes needed and qualities for leadership for future women ministers

No system or organisation is perfect. All organisations require ongoing reform and cultural change. The Uniting Church is no exception and it is within our DNA that regular reform and renewal is built into our ethos as a pilgrim people on the way as defined by the Uniting Church Basis of Union document. Following on from the previous chapter on women ministers' experiences, there were further responses around call and gifting. Equality in ministry was given by God so women ministers must be assertive about the respect expected and received. Another change needed was that we must call out poor attitudes towards women ministers when they are made, whether they be from men or women. Women ministers must want that leadership and act on it, by accepting the call and authority that God and the church have given them. We must educate the people we work with as a team that serves together as part of the body of Christ. Churches should not be holy clubs that set their own agenda. Some expressed that those women of the Uniting Church are privileged to be ordained, so we must celebrate that with women in other churches, who are not yet allowed to be ordained.

There were responses relating to the systems and structures within the church. We need more affirmative action to place women into more visible leadership roles and strategic roles; these include teaching in the theological colleges and working in Presbytery administrative, educational, and mission resourcing roles. It also perhaps includes the reestablishment of quotas on committees. This might also involve encouraging people to upskill and train for particular roles for the future. Our processes need to be transparent to ensure the best people are placed in leadership roles (rather than people being helicoptered into roles due to the old boys' network) through our placements system or when specialized roles are advertised.

Many responses centred around male colleagues needing to be educated or made more aware of their behaviour and language. These things include:

- sexist language and comments about their clothing or appearance;
- gatherings where it feels like the boys' club and you're the only woman present;
- challenging male entitlement;
- reporting bullying;
- naming passive aggressive behaviour;
- using the complaints processes more often rather than putting up with behaviour that does not align with the church's policy of being a safe church for all members and people regardless of age, gender, culture, and sexual orientation;
- educating men to realise when they are being disrespectful or trying to silence women;
- learning to step back and make room for women; and
- asking a question and then waiting for the answer instead of speaking over women.

In regard to support, some responses indicated more intentional mentoring could be provided by more experienced women ministers to those in earlier years, and this could be organised through presbytery networks. This is already a requirement of the third phase (first three years out) for new ministers, but informal networks are usually beneficial. The annual Women in Ministry retreat run for women ministry agents by Uniting Mission and Education in NSW/ACT has been a great gift for building these networks of support and care in recent years, and many women find deep support and encouragement and fun to sustain them. Some women with younger children felt they couldn't take up wider church roles due to family responsibilities, and this frustrated them at this stage of life.

As well as asking about changes that could be made to enable greater equality in leadership, the survey asked these women to identify the qualities that current and future women ministers need in order to be effective into the future. There was a huge list and much overlap so below is a list of the key qualities.

- Resilience
- Courage
- Persistence
- Patience
- Compassion
- Naming truth with integrity and kindness
- Being yourself without apology
- Owning who you are and having confidence in your calling
- Good emotional intelligence
- Focus on working in areas of strength and leaving the rest to others
- Hard headedness about work and family balance
- Willingness to evolve as the whole church has to evolve
- Be focused on God/confident in who we are in God, and point people to Christ

- Be flexible and adaptable
- Be able to integrate many skills and ideas
- Hold good boundaries
- Ability to work with various age groups
- Not to think you know everything but to have a willingness to learn and be taught by scholars, theologians, ministry colleagues, and the experience of other women
- Ability to network with the wider community
- Learning to speak up
- Stop working ourselves into the ground
- Claim the gifts God has placed within us and the natural talents that exist
- Become better equipped to deal with paternalistic and misogynistic people and be able to rest, recover, and rebuild
- Confidence and steadiness
- Train in conflict management and assertiveness
- Zeal for life
- Faith-based optimism
- Creative thinking
- Ability to delegate

What a list and what a great variety of qualities that can make up strong, faithful women leaders of the church for now and into the future. No one has all these qualities, but working as teams with lay people and church members, our church should be in great hands to create the future God is seeking for us. One of the comments from an anonymous respondent that stood out to me from the survey said, 'I love the women ministers in the Uniting Church. We are brave, resilient, run down a bit, having a go, faithful, smart, kind, thoughtful, strong and part of the answer to grow the faithful of God here in Australia.'

When asked what advice they'd give to younger women exploring their call to ministry now and in the next ten years, from a list of five responses the survey results were:

Know yourself well	77%
Remember your call and go for it	72%
Trust God and God will guide you	50%
Don't do it	13%

This reinforces many of the responses that were previously made back in 1994 about how women have coped with the challenges and developed capacities to persevere and thrive. The fact that some people felt these challenges would discourage younger women from entering into ministry into the future reflects some of the pain that some women have experienced in this work and the complexity and challenge of ministry leadership. In an ever-changing world and a church which is having to continue to adapt and reinvent itself for the future, women are possibly better placed to adapt than men due to their socialisation, but may not want to bear the cost of working within the institutional structures, whatever they may become. The more women who serve in higher levels of church leadership could enable the culture of the church to change and be more appreciative of the giftedness of women ministers. Over the past few years, our synod has been led by several strong women ministers, who have worked hard, and incrementally the culture of the church is beginning to change for the better.

A final anonymous quote from the survey that speaks to the complementarity of ministry leaders, both male and female, is helpful: 'Trying to have males and females the "same" in one sense is not helpful rather to celebrate our differences and recognise that together, we complement and strengthen each other because of those differences.'

We are all in this together and it should be together that we work out the ways to include and value everyone whom God has called into the lifelong leadership of God's church. There have been some great male minister colleagues I have journeyed with over the years, and we have much to learn from one another. As I look at the list on the previous page, I think it's time for all ordained ministry leaders to reflect more intentionally on their qualities for leadership and recover something of the wisdom therein, which may revitalise them to offer leadership into the 2020s and beyond.

CHAPTER 10

*Reclaiming the vision of equality
in leadership in Christ*

We have travelled a long way from the beginning of this book, from those looking back on the church's mission to those looking forward for what is yet to come. We have seen that feminist theology has broken open and created new ways of understanding God and the intrinsic equality before God of women and men. We have rediscovered in Jesus's ministry that women had and have their rightful place as disciples, servants, leaders of communities, and teachers. This rediscovery always involves border crossing for people to see and find a new way of living in Christ.

In subsequent chapters, we recalled that the strong, clear theological insights of women disciples and leaders has been quickly overrun by the reimposition of restrictions on women's ministries and subsequent subjugation of women as church leaders in the church's mainstream systems for about sixteen centuries.

We explored the notion of leadership and discovered that women have different ways or styles in which they lead. This contrasts to the more functional style that many male leaders exercise, leading to the dismissal of women's leadership as inferior and not real leadership. People lead in different ways regardless of gender. The more collaborative style, which is more commonly seen in women leaders, needs to be valued equally for the gift that it is in providing holistic ministry that is relationally based and building community rather than promoting competition.

The model of servant leadership which Jesus embodied is our model and the model which the Christian church needs to reclaim and develop its culture within all aspects of institutional and community life. How we hold authority and use it wisely, with kingdom values and intent, will be a good measure of our consistency and will colour and flavour our mission outcomes.

Reviewing the history of the ordination of women within the Uniting Church in Australia clarified the tough place that those early women and supporters worked in to break down the long-held barrier to the acceptance of women as gifted and called by God, to secure ordination to lead the church into the future, and to release their gifts for mission and ministry.

Whilst I am excited that 24 percent of ministers in the Uniting Church in NSW/ACT Synod are women today, I am disappointed that the percentage has decreased from 32 percent in 2016 when it should have been at least 50 percent by now. This is a challenge for current women ministers and for the future of the church to implement affirmative action strategies to include women in all roles available and all the councils of the church. There was a time when at least one third of all committees and task groups were women, but that measure has been eroded away over these past ten years. This is contrasted with the gender imbalance we see in most churches where 66 percent of members are women and 33 percent are men, yet male leadership is 70 to 90 percent in many churches. In the Uniting Church at present, 76 percent of ordained ministers are male, so serious work must be done to bring about a more even and diverse ministry team for the future.

There were many challenges for the early trailblazing women ministers, as I surveyed them in 1994. I was quite shocked that in 2021, twenty-five years after that initial research, many current women Ministers today were still reporting instances of being disrespected, marginalised, and not taken seriously, and that the younger the age group, the more overt was that discriminatory behaviour. That certainly resonated with my early experiences of congregational ministry leadership, and changed for the better once I moved into wider church roles, where there was more freedom to work creatively within the structures of the church. However, it seems that women have lost ground in this time, and the church is losing the benefit of gifted and skilled ministers who have to divert energy and focus to justify their leadership against gender attacks. This is not the way of Christ, and the church's mission will not flourish when there is division.

At a time when the church had to continue to adapt, change, and reinvent itself, women have been able to harness their creativity and flexibility to work effectively, in spite of much poor treatment. They have been awesome! Issues of women's power and authority under God not being accepted and respected continues to be a source of pain and heartache for many women ministers.

In spite of forty-four years of ordained ministry for women in the Uniting Church, some women feel disillusioned that the journey is still so difficult. As I said to some male leaders in a congregation in 2020, when I asked how many women ministers their congregation had called, I was told none. I replied, 'Why is it that after forty years of being a Uniting Church and being allowed to call women, we are still seen as a novelty? If you believe in that equality, then do something about it!'

These attitudes are deeply entrenched and will only change as we get on with the work of God's mission, call out unsafe behaviours, and remember that it is for God's church that we are servants. It is a mission in a church that we belong to, and it is not ours to play around with. We are to give our best to this church and to honour our sisters and brothers of faith, as Jesus would expect us to do. We have equality in Christ and should celebrate the women and men who have given their lives to serve God through leading others, meeting human need, providing spiritual guidance, and nurturing and fostering communities of people who love God through these actions.

As I complete this book, I am excited to report that the Uniting Church has just inducted its first ordained woman Assembly President in July 2021. I am delighted that Rev Sharon Hollis is the first ordained woman President of the Uniting Church in forty-four years, but why has it taken so long? She is the third woman to be elected as a President and head of the Uniting Church across Australia. There have only been two other lay women before her, one who has just completed three years and the other who was chosen over twenty years ago. We can celebrate the gifts of women leaders in the Uniting Church, but for a church that believes in the equality of women and men in ordained ministry, we have not lived up to our calling and have some more work to do from now into the future. I resonate with an article written by the Uniting Church Assembly General Secretary, Colleen Geyer back in 2017 for the 40th anniversary of the Uniting Church's formation. Geyer said that we are a church which celebrates women's leadership and must continue to allow and foster the many younger women who are now in leadership and will be called into leadership in the future.

Looking back, so much has changed and there has been much positive blessing that has come into the world through the ministry of faithful women leaders. We can't give up as there is too much at stake for the kingdom's causes to do that, but supporting one another in the journey and relying on the power of the Holy Spirit to empower us and accompany us is essential. It will also mean letting go of old ways and habits, and letting God do the new things that need to be done in our world with those who are committed to leading the church into the future, regardless of gender.

After twenty-five years of ordained ministry that I celebrated this year, it has been a privilege to have witnessed what God does in people's lives, how church communities transform, and how we adapt and embrace life's uncertainties with faith and courage. It has been a privilege to serve and lead God's people in worship, witness, and service and to make a unique contribution to the mission of God in the world. I look forward to the time when even more women will lead and serve in the Uniting Church and other denominations as ordained leaders. For the sake of those who still work and strive for the privilege of being ordained leaders within other parts of the Christian Church, may we and all women continue to offer our best inspired leadership and faithful service in the mission of God. May we be pointers to Jesus the Christ who brings love, healing, and wholeness to all who are looking for it.

APPENDIX 1

**Women in Ministry Survey 2021 -
For contribution to Rev Jan Reeve's book
*Feminist reflections on Mission & Leadership***

Thank you for your willingness to reflect on your ministry and complete this survey for me. No names will be mentioned, just seeking changing trends over the past 15-20 years.

Question Title

1. What type of ministry setting are you currently working in?

    ○ Congregation
    ○ Chaplaincy role
    ○ Presbytery role
    ○ Synod role
    ○ Assembly role
    ○ Other role

Question Title

2. How many years of ordained ministry have you completed?

   ○ 1-5 years
   ○ 5-10 years
   ○ 10-15 years
   ○ 15-20 years
   ○ 20-25 years
   ○ More than 25 years

Question Title

3. From when you began your ministry until now, have you experienced times of challenge related to your gender?

   ○ Yes
   ○ No

Question Title

4. Briefly describe the nature of the challenges you experienced?

Question Title

5. What strategies did you use to overcome these or what support enabled you to resolve them effectively?

Question Title

6. What are your greatest joys in ministry?

Question Title

7. What spiritual resources have enabled you to develop resilience to fulfil your call?

    ☐ Bible reading
    ☐ Regular prayer
    ☐ Journaling
    ☐ Professional/Pastoral supervision
    ☐ Retreats
    ☐ Colleagues
    ☐ Study
    ☐ Other

Question Title

8. Knowing what you know now about ministry leadership, what change is needed in the church to enable women ministers to fulfil their full potential as equals in leadership?

Question Title

9. What qualities do you believe women ministers need, in order to be effective in ministry into the future?

Question Title

10. What advice would you give younger women exploring their call to ministry for now and the next 10 years?

    ☐ Trust God and God will guide you
    ☐ Know yourself well
    ☐ Remember your call and go for it
    ☐ Don't do it!

BIBLIOGRAPHY
BY CHAPTERS

Chapter 1

Bosch, D.J., *Transforming Mission* (New York, 1993).

Dharmaraj, G.E., 'Women as border crossing agents: transforming the center from the margins', *Missiology*, 26 (1998), 55–66.

Chung, Sook Ja, 'Bible Study: Women's ways of doing mission in the story of Mary and Martha', *International Review of Mission*, 93 (2004), 9–17.

Johnson, Elizabeth, *She Who Is: The Mystery of God in Feminist Theological Discourse* (New York, 1992).

Kassian, M.A., *The Feminist Gospel*, (Illinois: 1992).

Lienemann-Perrin, C., 'The Biblical Foundation for a Feminist and Participatory Theology of Mission', *International Review of Mission*, 93 (2004), 17-35.

Long, Judi, 'Miss-iology meets Ms-Theology: Missiology and Feminist theology in creative interaction', *Mission Studies*, XIX (2002), 155-174.

Robert, D.L., "Women in World Mission: Controversies and challenges from a North American Perspective" *International Review of Mission* (2004) Vol 93, Iss 368, pp50-62

Schussler Fiorenza, E, *In Memory of Her* (London, 1983)

Schussler Fiorenza, E, *Discipleship of Equals* (New York, 1993)

Tucker R.A Chapter 3 "Women in Mission" in Phillips, J.M, & Coote, R.T.,

Toward the 21st Century in Christian Mission (Michigan, 1993)

Wilson Kastner, P, *Faith, Feminism and the Christ* (Philadelphia, 1983)

Chapter 2

Bosch, D.J., *Transforming Mission* (New York, 1993).

Dharmaraj, G.E., 'Women as border crossing agents: transforming the center from the margins', *Missiology*, 26 (1998), 55–66.

Chung, Sook Ja, 'Bible Study: Women's ways of doing mission in the story of Mary and Martha', *International Review of Mission*, 93 (2004), 9–17.

Johnson, Elizabeth, *She Who Is: The Mystery of God in Feminist Theological Discourse* (New York, 1992).

Kassian, M.A., *The Feminist Gospel*, (Illinois: 1992).

Lienemann-Perrin, C., 'The Biblical Foundation for a Feminist and Participatory Theology of Mission', *International Review of Mission*, 93 (2004), 17-35.

Long, Judi, 'Miss-iology meets Ms-Theology: Missiology and Feminist theology in creative interaction', *Mission Studies*, XIX (2002), 155-174.

Robert, D.L., "Women in World Mission: Controversies and challenges from a North American Perspective" *International Review of Mission* (2004) Vol 93, Iss 368, pp50-62

Schussler Fiorenza, E, *In Memory of Her* (London, 1983)

Schussler Fiorenza, E, *Discipleship of Equals* (New York, 1993)

Tucker, R. A., Chapter 3 "Women in Mission" in Phillips, J.M., & Coote, R.T.,

Toward the 21ˢᵗ Century in Christian Mission (Michigan, 1993)

Chapter 3

Anderson, T. D., *Transforming Leadership* (Massachusetts, 1992)

Becker, C. E., *Becoming Colleagues: Women and men serving together in faith* (San Francisco, 2000)

Becker, C. E., *Leading women: How Church women can avoid leadership traps and negotiate the gender maze* (Alban Institute, 2000)

Cairnes, M, *Approaching the Corporate Heart* (Sydney, 2003)

Dawswell, A, *Ministry Leadership Teams* (Cambridge, 2003)

Greenleaf, R. K., *The Power of Servant Leadership* (San Francisco,1998)

Hahn, C. A., *Growing in authority: Relinquishing control* (Alban Institute, 1994)

Higginson, R, 'Second wave, third wave,' in *Transforming leadership: A Christian approach to management* (London, 1996) 21-51

Manz, C. C., *The Leadership Wisdom of Jesus* (San Francisco, 1999)

Maxwell, J. C., *Developing the Leader within you* (Nashville, 1990)

McRae-McMahon, D, *Daring Leadership for the 21st century* (Sydney, 2001)

Skilton, C, *Leadership Teams* (Cambridge, 1999)

Sinclair, A, *Doing Leadership Differently* (Melbourne, 1998)

Tannen, D, *You just don't understand: Women and Men in conversation.* (New York, 2001)

Tymson, C, *Gender games: Doing business with the opposite sex* (North Sydney,1998)

Chapter 4

Bodycomb, J, 'Women in Holy Orders: the experience of the Uniting Church.'

Church Scene, 518, (28 July 1989) p5-6

Byrnes, J, 'Women clergy in leadership, A review of literature.' Australian Ministry, 2,3 (August 1990) p14-16

McMahon, D, 'The distinctive leadership of the minister.' Australian Ministry, 2,3 (August 1990) p6-8

McMahon, D, 'Power and authority in the Christian Church.' Australian Ministry 2,4 (Autumn 1990) p4-6.

Wood-Ellem, E, (ed) *The Church made whole.* (Melbourne, 1990).

Report of the Social Responsibility and Justice Committee April 1988

'Women in the Uniting Church in Australia.'

Report of the Social Responsibility and Justice Committee of the Assembly Commission for Mission. 'Why does the Uniting Church in Australia Ordain Women to the Ministry of the Word?' March 1990.

Chapter 5

Reeve, J, <u>CHF 115 Uniting Church Studies</u> -Report on Research assignment

'The Experience of Women Ministers in the Uniting Church' (Sydney, 1994) Unpublished

Acknowledgement of women Ministers contributing to that research in 1994.

Rev Norma Brown, Rev Maz Smith, Rev Diane Anderson (Stanton), Rev Leonie Hill & Rev Dr Rhonda White.

Chapter 8

Women in ministry Survey 2021 -For contribution to Rev Jan Reeve's book 'Feminist reflections on Mission & Leadership. See Appendix 1

Chapter 9

Joint Commission on Church Union *The Basis of Union* (Melbourne, 1971)

Chapter 10

Article by Colleen Geyer 'A church which celebrates women's leadership. https://assembly.uca.org.au/ 'A church which celebrates women's leadership.' Sept 28, 2017

Printed in the United States
by Baker & Taylor Publisher Services